AF485236

When Your Soul Finds You

ISBN:
Published by: Alegria Publishing
Book cover and layout by: @mckadamia

When Your Soul Finds You

ISLA MARTINEZ

The Soul

The Soul
is the place
where you can find
your truest,
most Divine self.

It is the center of your heart,
the oasis in your mind,
and the peace in your body.

Your Soul is a sanctuary
for your
joy and love.

You feel an intense
loving connection
with this entity.

At times you feel
it understands you
more than you
know yourself.

When you wake up in the morning
and ask God,
the Divine,
your Higher Self,
or the Universe,

What will today bring?

Your Soul brings you the answer.

Reflection

Before we get started,
I'd like to invite you
to take a few quiet moments
and reflect on what you hope
this journey will be for you.

Whether this time in your life
is a season of learning more
about your Soul,
reconnecting with your favorite
simple pleasures,

or you're hoping
to seek a new perspective,

this book is an invitation
for the beautiful and messy
parts of your life to co-exist as one.

I've read magical books
over the course of my 31 years
that have touched my Soul
in a way a book could only ever do.

In every one of those reads
I felt seen,
heard, and never judged.

Beautiful Soul,
please know
you are safe here.

While reading this book,
create a sacred space
for your reflections and ideas to live

so that you may look back
on this special time in your life
years from now
and remember
what your Soul was
feeling,
releasing,
creating.

A few things you can reflect on before diving in:

Who am I?

Is reflection
a part of my daily routine?

What am I hoping to
release from my heart?

Do I know my Soul?
Does my Soul know me?

Am I ready to deepen
my relationship with my Soul?

It's okay if you don't know the answers
to these questions at this moment.

Together, we'll get closer
to what our intentional
and loving answers may be.

Reflection has been a part of my life
from a really young age.
It's been my one
and true constant love.

It's a moment of silence
before I drink a cup of coffee
and ponder what my day
may bring.

It can also be found
in the beauty
that transpired
in specific conversations
or interactions
throughout my day.

Reflection can be simple,
yet always profound.

You don't need the perfect space
to invite it in.

It can be done
whenever and wherever
you choose;
it's all yours.

The act of reflection
will bring you closer
to your mind,
your heart,
and your Soul.

It's important
you invite it in
as often as you can.

Mornings

You have just woken up;
it's a new day.

You are alive.
You are existing.
You are breathing.
Affirm:
My Soul expands every
moment I choose love.

I feed my mind with words
that make me feel whole.

I am a compassionate Soul
with deep empathy for others.

I am loved, oh so deeply loved
by the people that matter the most.

I don't have anything to prove
to any job, any person, or any entity.
I am enough.

My dreams matter.
I am making progress.
I owe it to myself to keep going.

A new day brings me

renewal, joy, inspiration, and love.
*I am committed to being
the best me I can be.*

I know today will bring me everything I'm seeking,
I will allow myself to live this day as if I've never lived before.

What does my "dream" morning look like?

The best ideas
are born in silence,
in my own
 solitude
where everything feels
raw,
creative,
and free.

I have a deep appreciation

for the Souls
who create
quietly,
never seeking
 approval
from strangers
or ego.

It's in the quiet
where my truth
feels
the most clear.

Allow people
to meet
your Soul
(the real you)
at all times.

The Goddess in me,
sees the Goddess in you.

Maybe all we can really do is live
each day as if it's our last:

Our last hug.
Our last kiss.
Our last walk.
Our last book.
Our last coffee.
Our last conversation.
Our last page to write.

Would it really change anything?

We can always begin.

It's never too late to devour
this one beautiful life.

May these mantras invite renewal.

You can repeat these quietly
or out loud to yourself
and write them in your journal.

God and my Soul
are guiding me to Divine Love.

My strengths and gifts
are connected to infinite abundance.

The words I use in my everyday life
have the power to create more goodness.
I honor myself through the acts of self-love

I choose each day.
I am proud of myself
for showing up even in moments of fear or doubt.
I am the definition of joy.

I am an Artist.

I am ready to show the world who I really am.

I am on the right path.

I AM. I AM. I AM.

Everything changed
when I started my mornings with I AM.

I am alive.
I am capable.
I am beautiful.
I am abundant.
I am intelligent.
I am a Goddess.
I am expansive.

I AM–
Now, it's your turn.

Soul Gift

Each of us has a special gift,
a Soul gift.

We honor our Souls when we express ourselves
in every
breath, dance, laugh, smile, and cry.

When we finally feel ready
to show up
and serve our gifts,
we align with
our Soul's mission
and the greater collective.

*To know your purpose, your passion, your power
is the most sacred connection you'll have in your life.*

If you're still searching for yours,
you are in the best place you could be.

Overthinking it won't get you very far.
Your Soul asks that you spend more time *living*.

Travel opened my eyes to what the world had to
offer.
Walking allowed me to move forward with inten-
tion.
Journaling offered a space for my mind to renew.
Connecting with other Souls gave me clarity.
And *nature* quietly asked me to let go.

When the path is clear,
allow your Soul gift to show you the way.

My Soul Gift is...

From my journal–

I am in union with the love that exists in this
world.
I am a masterpiece in creation.
I am a magnet for authentic connection.

Sacred words fill my daily thoughts
so I may anchor myself to my Divine Soul.

The Past

Reminiscing on the past
can often bring intense emotions to the surface,
leaving us not wanting to reflect at all.

*But where would we be without
the memories and lessons of who we once were?*

My Soul has experienced
enlightenment,
awakening,
healing,
grief,
pain,
loss.

Only now do I know they were gifts for my Soul,

reminders to show me
life was never meant
to be easy.

I can honor
every past version of myself
with so much love and care,

and, at the same time,
rewrite my story.

My past
does not define
the Soul I am today.

Little Isla

I loved ballet
with my entire Soul.

I was a dancer for ten years
and spent the majority of my week
looking forward to Saturday,
so I could dance all of my worries away.

I loved the magic of getting ready:
Leotard, tights, bun, and bows—
a truly magical little ballerina.

Thinking back on those beautiful memories,
I only wish I could tell myself
to not worry so much about the little things.

I was never the thinnest one.
I was usually one of the only
brown girls in class,
and I often felt out of place.

But when it came time
to dance on the stage,
I would put on a show
that made my mom smile
big and bright;
she loved it as much as I did.

I share this with you to invite you to reflect on a
hobby, activity, or passion you had as a child.

*Is there a way you can invite this childhood love of
yours back in some way?
Your inner child
is longing to connect with you.*

Your inner child is longing to connect with you
today.
"Little me loved to..."

I vow to honor the woman
I was
before the world
told me
I had to change.

She is who I aspire to be:

A fearless Soul,
never letting
the world
dim her light.

Her bravery
will serve
as my guiding force
and leave perfection
at the door.

Thirty

They say life really starts when you turn thirty.
I believe it.

You can no longer hide from yourself
or the life
you've been told to follow.

Marriage,
kids,
a home.

All beautiful things,
but they're not everything.

If you're a woman in your thirties,
I applaud you
for simply
making it this far.

It's okay to still be figuring it out
at thirty, forty, fifty, sixty.

The most important thing you can do now
is start living for you.

If it feels good,
you're doing it right.

It's time
you place
joy
higher on your list.

Travel,
creativity,
or more hobbies,
your heart's truest desires.

Will you answer the call
to your own joy?

I Am the Best Person I Know

The people in my life are so lucky to know me.
They feel inspired by my magic.
My warm embrace is needed in their life.
When they think of me, they only feel love.

May this reach your heart on the days
you're feeling disconnected from
the essence of who you really are.

Allow yourself to embody these words.

When someone gives you your flowers,
write it down in a beautiful notebook.

Words carry meaning, and you deserve to
remember how people see you.

I'll be honest: it's incredible to be complimented
by anyone—
a stranger, a lover, a dear friend.

Imagine if you could feel that all the time?
With self-love you can.

"I am the best person I know."

Repeat this as many times as you need.

Be Gentle With Yourself

Today's version of you is showing up fully,
using all that you have to give.

Is a delayed timeline taking over your mind?

The truth is, nearly everyone feels
behind in some way or another.

We may voice our thoughts and lost dreams
to those closest to us,
opening a conversation that reveals
how alike we really are.

Delayed timelines can often cause a heartache
too large to bear.

Yet it is the *small and steady steps*
that will always guide us home.

All we can do is move forward
and trust that we are following the path
we're meant to be on.

There is only one you,
learning, healing, becoming.

It's possible others won't understand your story,
your timeline, your dreams,
or even your Soul.

If you're still finding your way *(we all are)*,
trust the unfolding.
Let go of the sadness, shame,
the quiet ache of comparison.

What is meant for you is written into your
becoming,
and it will meet you where you are.

Artists

We are all Artists.
Your mother, father,
friends, partners
are all creative Souls.

Painters, writers, dancers,
creators are among us
in every walk of life.

As children, they lived in their
creativity every single day,
free from judgement,
expectations, and comparison.

With every year that passed by,
their creativity may have slipped
from them bit by bit,
yet they still remain
an Artist at heart.

It can be difficult to see the people you love
lose their passion or spark
in the midst of all the things adulthood asks of us.

If this is you, or a friend you know;
all you need is 15 minutes a day—

space to feel it all
from your sacred Soul
and to create your art.

Keep it for yourself,
share it with someone you trust,
or post it online,
and see where it takes you.

*As long as you're creating,
the art is alive!*
I vow to create (more) Art.
My inner Artist is asking I start...

Mother Earth

I have so much gratitude for her.
She opens my heart
and heals my wounds.

It is in nature where things feel less heavy for me.
In her warm embrace is where I feel most
connected to the essence of my Soul.

Nature is the safest space
I know.

Everything we seek
is waiting for us on Earth
and will continue to live
forever in our Souls.

I'm humbly reminded my time here is limited.

Why not live in my truth?
I surrender to the plans I have made
and recreated
over and over and over again.

I'll leave it to God and the Divine,
and renew under the energy of the Sun.

Earthing

is an act of self-love

breathing
barefoot
the grounding
I deserve

my bare skin
rooted
in the earth
I'll one day
come to know

nature
my favorite language
I've ever learned

Gratitude

Thank you, Soul
Thank you, Soul
Thank you, Soul.

Repeat this three times
out loud,
preferably in front of a mirror.

Saying it three times in a row
makes it memorable,
significant,
and intentional.

You can make it your own.

Thank you, Soul, for your goodness.
Thank you, Soul, for your light.
Thank you, Soul, for your love.

Once you're done repeating it out loud,
write it in your journal.

This is how you speak life
into your Soul.

Your nervous system
is asking you to listen to the birds.

The chirps you hear
radiating from above
are a love song for your Soul.

If you take the time
to listen,
your heart will thank you later.

God created these magical beings
to invite
softness
into the everyday.

Their presence
is my favorite
form of mindfulness.

Your tears will always cleanse your
sensitive heart.

Imagine they're flowing into the ocean–
the same ocean
billions of Souls
love.

-Water

I've traveled to beautiful places in
Portugal, Spain, Italy, and France–
all gorgeous in their own way,
I hope to return soon.

But I must confess,
there's nothing quite like
the nature in Latin America.

I spent a summer in
San Miguel de Allende.
The birds
sang to me every morning
in a way that felt like
home away from home,
México lindo y querido.

The ocean in Cartagena
cleansed my Soul during a time in my life
when everything started to shift
for the better.

Our ancestors looked after the land,
and in return the animals, plants,
and people give and receive freely.

Latin America,
we honor your beauty.
Thank you.

Blue Mind

Sometimes all you need is a few minutes
to marvel at the sunlight
sparkling against the water,

a moment to connect with your blue mind–
peace and ease, guaranteed.

The sound of the waves
serves as music for your Soul.

You listen with intention
and remember you, too,
are vast, open, and
full of possibility.

Eldest Daughter

I am the older sister
I wish I had growing up.

My thirties
have shown me
the wisdom
I've carried
since adolescence
was always my greatest gift.

I didn't know if I was doing life right,
as a first-gen,
eldest daughter.

My prayers
were my guide.

I finally
feel worthy
of the title.

The one who gives advice,
teaches from the Soul,
and listens with caution and care.

Through the struggle
into my becoming,
my resilience
only ever sought
the acceptance of myself.

I know
everything
will work out
I'm the daughter
of immigrant parents
who have shown
there's always
a way

Have you ever taken a moment to reflect and honor your roots, family lineage, and the generations that came before you? Let's do that now. Write a letter to them.

Visualize Your Older Self

I often think
about who I'll be
when I'm older.

I visualize her
with impeccable taste,
and wrinkles that prove
she lived a full life.

Same girl–
only wiser
and somehow
even more beautiful.

I'd like to think she's full of joy,
loved,
and still has a deep appreciation
for learning.

God willing,
to be continued...

Renewal for My Soul

Waking up early to listen to the birds outside my window
Sunlight caressing my skin first thing in the morning
Hiking in Los Angeles on an early spring afternoon
Listening to Sade on the way to hot yoga
Healthy food to nourish my body
Sitting outside during a full moon
A morning without my phone
A consistent gratitude practice
Reading a book on philosophy
Transcendental meditation
Visiting a new coffee shop
Fresh fruit by the ocean
Buying myself flowers
Being around animals
Drinking fresh water
Bossa Nova
Community
True love
Walking
Solitude
Running

Sunday

I was born
on a Sunday

My Soul
was destined
for all things

Soft
Serene
Sacred

I hope my Soul always remembers
what it felt like to be out in nature
on a Sunday
in September.

-Virgo Soul

On Sundays,
I allow my Soul
to rest and renew
without judgment.

For the entirety of my twenties,
and now in my early thirties,
most Sundays have been reserved
for the softness in my Soul.

If this isn't something
you're used to,

I invite you to look after yourself
this Sunday.

Only gentle breaths
and slow movements.

You'll know your Soul
was guiding the way
when you feel renewed
at the end of the day.

I am light,
especially on a Sunday.

I am loved,
especially on a Sunday.

I am healthy,
especially on a Sunday.

I am blessed,
especially on a Sunday.

I am wealthy,
especially on a Sunday.

I am renewed,
especially on a Sunday.

I am beautiful,
especially on a Sunday.

I am good,
especially on a Sunday.

I am abundant,
especially on a Sunday.

I am peaceful,
especially on a Sunday.

I am everything
I want to be on a Sunday.

I'm from Southern California,
I feel like a Goddess
under the California Sun
on a Sunday
when I've just walked a few miles
for breakfast
and indulged in a green smoothie
or cafecito.

If you're a nature lover,
your best life is waiting for you
on the West Coast.

-California Soul

May your aura
radiate
only goodness
on a Sunday.

Friend,
I want you to know
that your worries,
anxiety, and sadness
make you
a real human
experiencing life
for the first time.

Yes, you are human,
and beyond your
humanness
you have a
Soul.

May you give your Soul
grace,
love,
patience,
nourishment,
and the *kindness*
you give to others.

111.
My intentions are manifesting with ease.
I am manifesting health, prosperity, abundance,
and all of my Soul's desires.

222.
I allow myself to surrender, even if it makes me
uncomfortable at first.
Breathe. Breathe. Breathe.

333.
The universe is supporting me in everything I do.
I must trust my intuition and inner wisdom at all
times.

444.
My angels and ancestors are always near me.
I am protected and divinely guided by God.

Higher Self

My higher self
is the girl
I was
as a child:

Whole.
Alive.
Connected.

The world allowed
her light
to shine.

As I got older,
I'd find glimpses of her,

mostly in whispers,
when she felt at home.

It's up to me
to call her in,
when my creativity
needs her.

I know
she still
lives
within me now.

Higher Self Exercise

Close your eyes
and prepare to be still for as long as you need.
This moment is for you,
no one else but you.

Breathe in and out.
In and out.
In and out.
Slower and deeper.

With every breath you are releasing
anything that no longer serves your Higher Self.
This can be any fear, anxiety, depression, or stress
you may be feeling.

Our Higher Selves
require us to release these things
so we can fully be *free*.

Your Higher Self
is the version of you
that is authentic, majestic, fearless,
passionate, artistic, abundant, and full of magic.

You know this version of you exists,
I know you do.

Your Higher Self
is deeply connected
to your Soul,
to the Divine,
to Light,
to God.

With every breath,
you call in
only what your Soul
truly desires.

Your big dreams, intentions, and manifestations
you've been putting off
deserve your full attention right now.

*With your eyes closed and your hands over your heart
repeat the following:*

Miracles are pouring down on me.

I must always
trust my inner knowing.

I am open to the guidance
my Higher Self offers me daily.

Higher Self,
I love you.

What does your Higher Self look like? Visualize your Higher Self and write about it in detail.

Transcendental Meditation

The first time I meditated,
I realized
how beautiful
the quiet can be.

I learned that
meditation
can be done
anytime
you're seeking
the light within.

My teacher
praised
how this art
can shift
anxiety to peace.

And in those first moments
of stillness,
my mind told me,

It's okay. You're safe.
You don't have to worry.
Here is where you let it all go.

Once I heard those words,
I knew meditation
was my friend, my ally
the quiet my Soul was asking for.

Senses

My senses calm my anxious mind
and plant my body in a way that feels
grounding and ever so present.
I see,
   I hear,
      I smell,
         I taste,
            I touch.

Anytime you're feeling burdened
by the weight of the world,
connect to the following:

To See.
What do I see of beauty around me?

To Hear.
What do I hear that brings forth curiosity?

To Smell.
Are there any aromas that smell exquisite?

To Taste.
Can I taste something new I've never had before?

To Touch.
Will I allow myself this moment to be still—
touch my hand to heart and let go of it all?

Soul Clearing

Inviting sacred energy
into my daily rituals
cleanses my Soul.

Scents of white sage
while I'm journaling,
relaxed muscles in hot yoga,
serene thoughts in meditation.

I didn't know feeling sacred
could feel so free.

Beneath my skin
lies a Soul waiting for
a transformative rebirth:

releasing the past,
speaking words of affirmation
surrounded by the gifts of nature,
and opening the path
to renewal.

The steady rhythm of my heart
craves a Soul that is connected.

How do I get there?

By anchoring into love
with every part of my being.

By igniting the fire within
when I feel like there is nothing left.

By merging with miracles,
and rising above the noise.
By coming alive, fully.

I meet my Soul
face to face
everytime I watch
a beautiful sunset.

I invite you to watch a sunset at a lookout, park, or beach near you.
Write about your experience with as much detail as you can.
Connect to all of your senses: sight, hearing, smell, taste, touch.

Renew Your Soul at These Sacred Spaces in Southern California

The Huntington Library in San Marino.
For the Soul who wants a little bit of everything:
a walk in the gardens, a slow hour at the library,
and a cafecito moment at the cafe.

Pointe Dume in Malibu.
For the sunset lovers:
watching golden hour by the water
alone or with the company of someone
you don't have to perform for.

Lake Shrine Meditation Gardens in Pacific Palisades.
These gardens are where you're meant to be still–
embrace solitude.
If you want to spend quality time in meditation,
or awaken your heart to inner peace,
you're welcome no matter which religion you
follow.

Casa Romantica in San Clemente.
For the romantic who needs a short getaway.
Visit this gem when you want to feel like
you're somewhere completely new.
Turn off your phone, feel the crisp ocean
breeze on your skin, and love on your Soul.

The Getty Villa in Pacific Palisades
When you need to step away from your home or
the constant chaos of the big city.
Enjoy every corner, with your camera in hand,
and allow the art to move you.

Visiting these sacred spaces allowed me to spend
hours writing, walking, and connecting to my
creativity.
I hope you find the magic in them just as I did.

Nature Reflections

When you find yourself
needing to move
from your current situation,

*move your body
so you can free your Soul.*

Mindful movement
has helped me get out of my head
and invite action
into my life

every. single. time.

You aren't meant to be trapped
in your discomfort or anxiety.

A reset is calling you now,
and you must say yes.

Sign up for the cycle class.
Stretch your muscles.
Walk with a friend.
Go out for a run.

As long as you prioritize
moving your body,
you'll keep going for more.

Go out for a walk in nature and keep your journal close.
Write about your experience in nature.

I am Divinely guided–
today, tomorrow, siempre.

What if everything I am seeking
is seeking me too?

Self-awareness is how you better understand the
person you are.
Study your mind, your thoughts, your actions
and try to piece yourself together as best as you can.

It's time to dig deeper.
I think you know it, too.

What are you avoiding?
What are you seeking more of?

I always find healing when I uncover a part of my-
self I haven't met yet.
It's never been difficult for me to analyze myself;
I'm an observer at heart.

So, this is your invitation to look at everything you
are and do.
Treat it like an art you love.

To show up as our truest selves in this world,
we must know who we are.

On a hot, mid-summer day,
I came across a delicate flower
I don't see often:
the lotus.

I was feeling pretty tired,
but I had a pre-booked
ticket to a garden in Los Angeles.

When I saw her
rising above the water,
I knew it was my sign
to find the deeper meaning
before I moved on.

A lotus usually requires
a full sun
to bloom.
And when they're in bloom,
they only live about three to five days.

This was new information to me,
and it felt deeply personal considering

I was standing
right in front of her.

Her bloom may be short,
yet her beauty is
everlasting,
majestic,
and rooted in love.

It was on this day that
I promised myself
to transcend above it all and
embrace the
Divine Feminine
in my Soul
where the lotus flowers grow.

Creativity Cures Criticism

Julia Cameron, an author who has deeply inspired me
over the last few years,
profoundly shares in her book, *The Artist's Way,*
that creativity cures criticism.

Many of us will have moments
when we abandon ourselves,
disconnect from our Souls,
and give in to the words
that are not true to who we are.

My invitation for you:
talk to your inner critic like you would a friend.

Make peace knowing you're doing your best–
your Soul deserves more compassion and self-love.

In yourself,
your work
and art.

Release the criticism,
and instead, honor and nourish
your inner creative today.

Songs to Listen to on a Sunday

Soledad y Mar (feat. Los Macorinos) by Natalia Lafourcade
Mercy Mercy Me (The Ecology) by Marvin Gaye
Knockin' On Heaven's Door by Bob Dylan
Closer by Goaple
Kiss of Life by Sade
Sunshine by Cleo Sol
I've Seen It by Olivia Dean
Turn Me On by Norah Jones
My Girl by The Temptations
Lovely Day by Bill Withers
Work by Charlotte Day Wilson
River by Leon Bridges
On & On Erykah Badu
Dreams by Fleetwood Mac
Golden by Jill Scott
Compartir by Carla Morrison
Fade Into You by Mazzy Star
A Sunday Kind Of Love by Etta James
It's Too Late by Carole King
Put Your Records On by Corrine Bailey Rae
I Say a Little Prayer by Aretha Franklin
Matilda by Harry Styles
Man at the garden by Kendrick Lamar
Got to Be Real by Cheryl Lynn
Devotion by Earth, Wind & Fire
Vibrate by Londrelle, Lala Delia
Intergalactic Janet by Ley Soul
Godspeed by Frank Ocean

The Art of Listening

I love listeners.
Those who always want to hear the full story.
The ones who ask more questions,
don't interrupt when you're speaking with passion,
and see you as you want to be seen.

In a time when technology is taking over our days,
conversations, and interests,
I would much rather spend time with listeners.

I asked myself recently,
"Am I still a good listener?"

I couldn't quite come up with an answer
in the moment,
and I took a few days to sit with myself
as honestly as I could.

I considered the following:

Am I allowing for a safe space?
What is their demeanor when speaking to me?
Am I asking the right questions?
Do they leave smiling?

I contemplated on these questions for few days
and my final answer:

I listen carefully—with love and intention.
I always do my best to show up
in my conversations
with honesty, sincerity and humility.

*Listening is one of my favorite ways
to connect.*

Who is the best listener you know? Why?
Share this journal entry with them.

Luxuries Are Born in the Heart

For many,
luxury is money,
fame, and wealth.

I'd like to believe
it's a little bit more than that.

Luxury
is born in the most meaningful place of all,
the heart.

Taking yourself out on a walk when you first wake
up,
luxury of health.

Visiting a bookstore and leaving with a new read,
luxury of knowledge.

The privilege of paying all your bills on time,
luxury of abundance.

Spending a day reconnecting with your joy,
luxury of solitude.

Praying in the morning for the chance to start
anew,
luxury of gratitude.

You have beautiful luxuries
waiting to be discovered.

I hope one day you meet a miracle
that shows you we are made of stars.

The new era you're about to embark on
will be the best one
you've lived yet.

Your mornings will feel sweeter;
every ritual
sacred and intentional.

Feeling behind will
no longer control you
as you're finally
taking up space.

You're seen and heard in
everything you do.
It feels like you're
catching your breath.

You're living from a place of magic,
not fear.

You're doing everything
you said you would
even if it feels
like it doesn't make sense.

You're in your flow state–
and your Higher Self
is pulling the reins.

People are asking you,
"How are you doing it?"

Your answer?
You're meant for more.
Do it all
messy, imperfect, and afraid.

More

Today is the day you ask for more.
God is waiting to give you all you deserve.

More abundance.
More opportunities.
More aligned partnerships.

The more you've been waiting for.

Amor

My favorite ways to say
I love you

Knowing your coffee order
by memory

Offering a smile
to show you I care

Spending my day off
doing something you love

Answering the call
no matter how busy the day is

Dedicating a morning
writing session in your name

Acts of service–
how my Soul loves.

My favorite ways to say I love you are...

84

You are the goodness
you see in others.

With love–

your Soul
will deeply
embody
ease,
intention,
and devotion.

You deserve this,
beautiful Soul.

Thank you for reminding me who I was
when I felt my spark was gone forever.

The light you see in me
is a reflection of the light
within your own Soul.

May you always shine bright
and feel deeply loved.

–Amor

"When you are real and honest,
the hands of God touch your heart."

–Words shared with me by a stranger at a cafe

The Student

Dreams take time—
all beautiful things do.

One day, you wake up and finally decide
to keep the dream alive.
You must keep going,

even if you have more
questions than answers.

Every pivot and transition
you've moved beyond,
is a reminder
to trust in the process.

You've learned
everything
you need to know.

A student of life
must also take action.

By saying yes
to the dream,
you'll come to know
it's closer than you imagined.

It's going to get much better,
I promise.

The good is almost here—
it's so close, I can feel it for you.

If no one else has told you this—
please don't give up now.

You've come so far,
we all see it.

Your parents, loved ones,
best friends,
mentors and teachers,
always believed in you;
they still do.

Take as long as you need,
a day, a week, a month, a year.

And when you're ready, we'll be here.

Do you hear the standing ovation?
It feels good, doesn't it?
The hard part is over.

Joy has been calling for you.

You were so missed
never forgotten
only ever loved.

Spend more time *giving* to your natural strengths.

You'll find life is easier
when you know
what you are good at.

Not what you can perfect, but
what *naturally* comes easy to you.

Don't overcomplicate it.

Here are a few ideas you can start with:

Motivating someone to finally pursue that dream.
Organizing and creating new systems.
Analyzing numbers into clear data.
Staying calm when others turn angry.
Conceptualizing a business idea.
Adapting to a new environment.
Creating art of any form.
Making a stranger laugh.
Building strong relationships.
Leading a team.

Your connection to these natural strengths
will help you embody your Soul Gifts.

What are my natural strengths?

This is the year you're done saying,
"Maybe tomorrow."

Because tomorrow
always comes,
and you're left
with regret
at the end of the day.

This is it.
Today is your chance
to start.

You don't have to
have it all figured out.
You just have to
take that first step.

Will you start today?
The leap will change you for the better.

You can start.
I know you can.

Find the mirror closest to you,
and prepare yourself for what's to come.
Look at your eyes,
your beautiful, God-given eyes.
And when you're ready,
these are the words you'll say:

I am ready.
The world has been waiting
for me all along.

Your
SOUL
knows
you
by
name

Soul to Soul

May you find the beauty in journaling,
no matter the season you're currently in.

I discovered the art of journaling at a very young age,
and it was one of the only things that felt like
true magic at the time. That still rings true for me
today.

Please keep the following in mind when you're jour-
naling:

- Always keep an open mind, heart, and Soul.

- You don't have to be a writer to start this practice.

- Remember to write when you're feeling both good
and bad, not just when you need to vent.

- No, you don't have to share your writing with
anyone else.

- It's okay if you haven't written in days, weeks, or
months– start today.

- Journaling is not a practice you have to perfect.

- If you're feeling stuck on what to write about, try
going outside. I have always been the most inspired
in nature.

- Yes, it's a beautiful thing to follow a prompt, but
it's not required.

- You don't have to have a pretty or aesthetic journal. Use the following pages in this book as your starting point.

Please have fun! Your Soul deserves to find joy in journaling.

I am finally ready to...

El amor es...

El amor es...

In nature, who am I?

Today is the day I will finally turn the page on...

I awaken my Soul by...

I awaken my Soul by...

When was the last time I was in AWE of myself?

In which ways have I been told I'm magic?

Lately, I have been asking myself...

How can I actively be a better listener to a loved one this week?

I find real joy in...

I find real joy in...

What is the most beautiful thing I see (in nature) right now?

Lately, I've been dreaming of...

Thank you, God, for...

Thank you, God, for...

What does the word "transcend" mean to me?
Write on anything that may come up for you.

What is energizing my Soul in this season of life?

I love how you...

I love how you...

If you could visit any place in the world, where would you go?
Visualize your Soul at this place.

Little by little, I've been...

Who is your favorite artist? How does this artist inspire you?

Write a love letter to your Soul.

Write a love letter to your Soul.

Thank you

My Soul guided me to write these words
in my journal and share them with you.

I hope these reflections and prompts
have supported your own healing journey.

If you take anything away from this book,
let it be that your Soul knows you by name.

Spend more time in nature.

Journal when you can.

Your intuition will always be your best guide.

I encourage you to read *When Your Soul Finds You*
as you are drinking your morning cafecito,
admiring a sunset,
or journaling in your sacred space.

May your connection to your Soul find you
and meet you where you are, siempre.

Thank you for sharing space with me.

About the Author

Isla Martinez is an author, speaker, and writing workshop facilitator.

An advocate of "journaling for the Soul," she draws from experiences and reflections to inspire a guided journey of renewal and awakening.

Her debut book, *When Your Soul Finds You,* seeks to bring authentic connection and community to hearts and Souls far and wide.

Isla graduated from California State University, Fullerton with a Bachelor of Arts in Communications and a Minor in Cinema and Television Arts.

A coffee aficionado with a wanderlust for nature, her next destination is only a dream away.

You can book Isla for your next workshop, speaking engagement, or event.

Visit her Instagram to access the audiobook and more of her Soul reflections.

Instagram: @SoulSesiones
Email: connectwithisla@gmail.com